PRODUCTION BY
Sabistar Pty Ltd (AUS) and The Verity Leadership Institute

CONTACTS
SABISTAR
studio@sabistar.com
www.sabistar.com

THE VERITY LEADERSHIP INSTITUTE
www.verityleadership.com

Limits of Liability/Disclaimer Of Warranty

____/____/________

____/____/______

_____/_____/________

_____/_____/_______

____/____/______

____/____/______

_____/_____/_________

_____/_____/________

_____/____/________

____/____/______

_____/_____/_________

____/____/________

____/____/______

_____/_____/________

____/____/____

___/___/_____

_____/_____/________

_____/_____/________

____/____/______

____/____/______

___/___/_____

___/___/______

_____/_____/_________

____/____/________

____/____/________

____/____/______

____/____/______

_____/_____/________

_____/_____/_________

______/_____/________

_____/_____/_________

____/____/________

___/___/______

_____/_____/________

_____/____/_______

_____/_____/________

_____/____/_______

____/____/______

_____/_____/________

____/____/______

_____/____/_______

_____/_____/_________

_____/_____/________

_____/_____/_____

_____/_____/________

______/_____/__________

_____/_____/________

_____/____/_______

_____/_____/________

_____/_____/_________

_____/_____/_________

____/____/________

_____/_____/________

_____/_____/_________

___/___/______

____/____/______

___/___/_____

______/_____/_________

_____/_____/________

____/____/________

___/___/______

_____/____/_______

_____/____/_______

____/____/________

____/____/________

_____/_____/________

____/____/______

_____/____/_______

_____/____/_______

_____/____/________

_____/_____/________

____/____/______

_____/____/_______

_____/_____/________

____/____/______

_____/_____/_________

_____/____/_______

_____/____/_______

___/___/_____

_____/____/________

_____/____/________

_____/_____/________

____/____/______

_____/_____/_________

____/____/________

____/____/________

_____/____/________

_____/_____/________

_____/_____/_________

_____/_____/________

_____/_____/_________

_____/____/_______

_____/_____/_________

_____/____/_______

____/____/______

_____/_____/_________

____/____/________

____/____/______

____/____/________

___/___/______

_____/____/_______

____/____/________

____/____/______

_____/____/________

____/____/______

____/____/________

____/____/______

_____/_____/_________

_____/____/________

_____/_____/_______

_____/_____/_______

_____/_____/________

____/____/______

_____/____/_______

____/____/______

_____/_____/________

___/___/_____

______/_____/_________

_____/_____/________

_____/_____/________

_____/_____/_________

_____/____/_______

_____/_____/________

_____/_____/________

____/____/______

_____/_____/_________

_____/_____/_________

_____/_____/_________

_____/_____/_________

____/____/______

_____/_____/________

_____/____/_______

____/____/______

____/____/________

_____/_____/_________

____/____/________

_____/_____/________

____/____/________

_____/_____/________

____/____/________

_____/_____/_________

____/____/______

____/____/________

____/____/______

_____/_____/________

____/____/________

___/___/___

___/___/_____

___/___/_____

____/____/______

_____/_____/________

____/____/______

____/____/______

_____/_____/_________

_____/____/_______

____/____/____

____/____/________

_____/_____/________

_____/_____/_________

_____/_____/________

____/____/______

_____/_____/_________

___/___/_____

____/____/______

_____/_____/________

_____/_____/_________

_____/_____/________

____/____/________

_____/_____/________

_____/_____/_________

_____/_____/________

____/____/________

____/____/______

_____/____/_______

_____/_____/________

___/___/_____

_____/_____/________

______/______/__________

_____/_____/_________

_____/_____/________

_____/_____/_________

____/____/________

_____/_____/_________

_____/_____/_______

___/___/______

_____/_____/________

_____/____/_______

____/____/______

____/____/________

_____/_____/_________

____/____/______

_____/_____/_________

_____/____/_______

_____/____/_______

_____/____/_______

_____/_____/_________

_____/_____/_________

______/_____/________

____/____/________

_____/____/_______

_____/_____/________

____/____/______

____/____/______

_____/_____/________

___/___/_____

_____/_____/_________

_____/_____/_______

_____/_____/________

_____/_____/________

_____/_____/_________

____/____/________

___/___/______

_____/_____/________

_____/_____/_________

_____/_____/_________

_____/_____/________

_____/_____/________

___/___/_____

_____/_____/________

_____/_____/________

_____/_____/________

______/_____/_________

___/___/_____

_____/_____/________

___/___/______

____/____/______

____/____/______

____/____/______

_____/_____/________

___/___/_____

____/____/______

_____/_____/________

_____/_____/________

_____/_____/________

_____/_____/________

____/____/______

____/____/________

____/____/______

_____/____/_______

____/____/______

www.ingramcontent.com/pod-product-compliance
Lightning Source LLC
LaVergne TN
LVHW040826090826
845145LV00001BA/210